Min

100+ Amazing Mindfulness Tips, Exercises & Resources. Bonus: 200+ Mindfulness Quotes to Live By! (Mindfulness for Beginner's, Mindfulness Meditation, Yoga & Mindfulness, Anxiety & Mindfulness)

Kevin Gise © 2015

Disclaimer:

Introduction

First off, thank you for purchasing my book "Mindfulness: 100+ Amazing Mindfulness Tips, Exercises & Resources. Bonus: 200+ Mindfulness Quotes to Live By! (Mindfulness for Beginner's, Mindfulness Meditation, Yoga & Mindfulness, Anxiety & Mindfulness)". By purchasing this book you've shown that you're serious about self improvement and trying to become your best self.

Mindfulness is an idea that's been around for a long time and has begun to gain more traction with the general public over the past few years. It's a way of thinking, and a set of techniques, a person can use to help improve their life in a meaningful way. Perhaps, you feel cut off from your feelings or constantly overwhelmed by them. Maybe, you keep falling from one bad situation to another, or you're having difficulty interacting with those around you. Whatever you're set of circumstances, the information in this book can help you.

Practicing mindfulness and making it a part of your daily life will let you regain control of your feelings and behavior. It will empower you to overcome any adversity that comes your way. It will improve your overall sense of well being, while also calming your mind and spirit.

This book will touch on a lot of different mindfulness topics, along with providing you some resources and inspirational quotes to help you during the course of your journey. This is not a change that happens overnight. It will take some time and diligence on your part. However, the work you put in is well worth it in the long run.

I'm excited to begin. Let's get started!

Chapter One: An Introduction to Mindfulness

In this chapter, you will learn:

- An Introduction to Mindfulness

- The Benefits Of Mindfulness

An Introduction to Mindfulness

What is mindfulness? Well, mindfulness is the awareness of your mind at any given moment. What does that mean in practical terms? It means being able to step back from having any type of immediate response to a situation, and being aware of how you feel, what you're thinking, along with being aware of what is happening in your surroundings. Mindfulness is paying attention to both yourself and the world going on around you. It's about experiencing things instead of just witnessing them happen.

Mindfulness has a few different components that I'll break down and discuss a little further.

Being In The Moment

This is the ability to live in the present, fully aware that you cannot change the past, knowing that you're future has yet to be written. Both your thoughts and feelings are valuable and valid because they are occurring in the moment.

Attentiveness

This is the ability to really begin noticing what is going on around you. It can be something as simple as feeling the texture of the floor with your feet, or feeling your heart beating.

Being Non-Judgmental

One of the goals of becoming mindful is being aware of things without judging them as bad or good automatically. Being aware of the entire situation going on around you will allow you to take appropriate action.

Compassion

It can be easy to give in to our negative thoughts and feelings about not only our self but about the other people around us. To show compassion is to recognize your own limitations and fallibility as a person, and to show forgiveness and understanding for both yourself and others.

Being Non-Reactive

This is similar to being non judgemental. You don't want to immediately react to a situation the moment it occurs. I'm not saying don't react at all. I'm saying that you want to take a moment to assess the situation and experience the moment that is going on around you. Once you've done that you can then act appropriately.

Some skeptics may say what if you're in immediate danger, don't you want to react immediately? The answer I always give, is in the vast majority of situations you'll encounter throughout your lifetime, having the ability to stay in control of your actions and emotions will allow you to much better assess and respond to any situation then you' be able to do if you were simply reacting based on fear.

The Benefits Of Mindfulness

In this section I'm going to discuss some of the many benefits associated with living a more mindful lifestyle. These benefits have all been researched extensively and have empirical data to back up their beneficial claims.

Reduced Negative Thinking

Studies have shown that mindfulness helps reduce rumination and negative thinking. In addition to this, people who practice mindfulness experience fewer symptoms of depression.

Stress Reduction

There's been over 40 medical studies that have shown that practicing mindfulness will help to alleviate stress. It's been shown that practicing mindfulness on a daily basis can alter your cognitive processes, helping to decrease both anxiety and stress long term.

Improved Memory Function

Being mindful will help to boost your working memory. Studies have shown that people who participate in mindfulness meditation have substantial increases in their memory capacity over time.

Focus

Another benefit, is an enhanced ability to focus and an increased ability to suppress any distracting information. Mindfulness has been shown to correlate directly with better attentional functioning and cognitive flexibility.

Less Emotional Reactivity

People who practice mindfulness develop skills to become more self observant than those around them. It also allows people to better handle negative or stressful situations without letting their emotions overcome them.

Stronger Relationships

Several studies have shown that mindfulness has a positive affect on relationship satisfaction. Being mindful allows you to respond well under relationship stress instead of lashing out. It also allows you to communicate your emotions better to your partner. Mindfulness has also been shown to help protect a person from the stressful emotional effects that occur during relationship conflict.

Besides the benefits listed above, mindfulness has also been shown to help enhance a person's morality, self insight, fear modulation, intention and immune functioning. As you can see the benefits of being mindful are abundant and well worth the time and effort you put into practicing it.

Chapter Two: How to Get Started On The Path to Mindfulness

In this chapter, you will learn:

- How to Get Started On The Path to Mindfulness

- Simple Meditation Techniques for Beginner's

How to Get Started On The Path to Mindfulness

So you've decided you want to become more mindful. However, you're not quite sure how to go about achieving this. Well, in this section I'll go over some of the different steps you can take in order to start down the path to leading a life of mindfulness.

There are several different practices and disciplines that help to cultivate mindfulness. A few of these include tai chi, yoga, qigong and meditation. All of these are wonderful methods. Most of my personal experience lies in mindfulness meditation and yoga, so those are the areas that I will concentrate on primarily in this book.

There are two main forms of meditation along with various other types that focus on certain areas we want to work on. I'll briefly go over both main forms and the various types so that you understand the differences between them.

Two Main Forms of Meditation

1. Concentration Meditation – This type of meditation is where you narrow your attention and focus on your breath along with an object, image, or sound. You do this in order to help calm your mind and allow for more clarity and a higher awareness to emerge.

2. Mindful Meditation – This type of meditation is where you open up your awareness and attention to all sensations, thoughts, feelings, sounds, smells and images without judgment or evaluation.

Various Meditation Types

1. Awareness Meditation – This is the practice of moment to moment observation of your surroundings and the world as they truly happen to be. This type of meditation promotes a stable, clear awareness of one's thoughts without any judgment.

2. Loving Kindness Meditation – This kind of meditation is a heartfelt wish of happiness and well being to not only yourself, but extending out to everyone else around you. This meditation helps to reinforce our emotions of compassion, kindness, love and appreciation.

3. Japa Meditation – This type of meditation is a repetition of a Sanskrit term or mantra while using the rotation of a rosary or beaded Mala. This meditation is considered to be extremely effective for tension and stress.

4. Transcendental Meditation TM – This kind of meditation has been widely researched and uses a practiced seven step program that gives each of its students a personal mantra or sound using a comfortable seated technique with eyes closed.

5. Passage Meditation – This type of meditation uses inspirational and spiritual passages, that are supported by seven different disciplines. These disciplines fit any non religious or religious philosophy, enabling a practitioner to stay kind, calm, and focused.

6. Vipassana Meditation or Insight Meditation – This kind of meditation practices mindfulness and practices shedding a light on the subtlest workings of our mind. This is done in order to bring the true nature of our reality into sharper focus. This allows us to have a much deeper interconnection between our body and mind.

7. Yoga – The benefits of practicing yoga are both clear and very conclusive. This type of movement meditation, using relaxation techniques and breathing, allows you to drastically reduce stress and tension from both your mind and body.

8. Qigong & Tai Chi - These art forms speak to people who enjoy martial arts and want to learn meditation and relaxation techniques. These techniques are very popular among seniors.

I'm also a big fan of walking meditation. I find it's something I can easily weave into my daily life. I keep my walks simple, however, some people prefer elaborate labyrinth walking or even trying their hand at meditative dance. I've yet to do either so I can't comment on how effective they are in relation to just a normal walking meditation.

Simple Meditation Techniques For Beginners

Most traditional forms of meditation come from some type of older religious origins. However, you don't need to be a monk in order to reap the rewards meditation provides.

What form of meditation you decide is best for you will depend on your purpose and preference. For instance, I stick to mindful meditation, walking meditations, and yoga. I found those are what work best for me in my life.

In this section, I'm going to discuss simple ways you can begin opening your mind to meditation. I'll go into mindfulness exercises and mindfulness meditation in later chapters. These are just a few ways you can begin practicing immediately while doing ordinary things. The purpose of these suggestions are to start learning how to begin slowing down and calming your mind.

Breath Awareness Mediation

This is a very effective form of meditation all by itself. Let's go over how you can begin to start practicing this form of meditation.

First, try sitting upright in a relaxed position keeping your spine straight. Begin by closing your eyes. Take a few moments to yourself and simply be. Notice whatever you happen to be experiencing, in that particular moment, without taking any action on it.

Once you've allowed yourself to get settled in, start noticing your breath as it both leaves and enters your body. Don't try and manipulate your breathing patterns in any way. Experience your breathing and feel how the air moves in and out of your nose along with how your body moves when breathing.

At times your mind will begin to wander away from your breath. That's completely normal, it doesn't matter. It's actually a part of this meditation! If you notice you're no longer only observing your breath you can easily focus your attention back to it when your mind wanders.

Let each of your experiences, emotions, thoughts, and bodily sensations continuously come and go, while staying in the background of your awareness of your breath. Notice how these things all come and go, effortlessly and automatically, like your breath.

Over time, you'll learn the different tendencies your mind has. You'll see how it tries to hold onto certain experiences, while resisting others. Letting your mind settle down naturally will allow you to recognize these tendencies, while giving you the opportunity to let go of them and any of the negativity attached to them.

Audio Or Guided Meditation

It's also possible to find a serene and calm peace of mind while doing mundane activities. Things that you find to be boring or routine can be changed into mindfulness exercises you can use for deeper self relaxation.

For example, I enjoy walking so I turned the time I used on my walks into time I can practice walking meditation. You can meditate while doing a variety activities. Anything from sports like biking and swimming to hobbies like painting and gardening.

Another simple way to begin meditating is by seeking out relaxing activities when you begin to feel stressed. Listening to some music, writing in a journal, and reading are all good examples. These activities all work in a similar way. They help to focus your mind while also lowering your beta brain activity. This helps to naturally put your mind in a more meditative state.

Guided relaxation meditations are great form of meditation that uses instruction, imagery, stories, natural sound effects and music to help you focus, relax and follow along. You can find these offered in every format imaginable from CD's and DVD to MP3 downloads and cassette tapes.

Another popular form of meditation is Brain Wave Entrainment. These audio CD programs have been gaining in popularity. This form of meditation uses binaural beats to help synchronize your brain waves and then alter the brain wave frequencies into a specific state of consciousness. What this does is enable a person to reach a deeper state of meditation very quickly.

The different forms and methods of mediation are almost endless. You're really only limited by your imagination. The sooner you get started the sooner you'll start to enjoy the simple pleasure of existing.

Chapter Three: 11 Mindfulness Exercises to Get You Started!

In this chapter, you will learn:

- 11 Mindfulness Exercises to Get You Started!

11 Mindfulness Exercises to Get You Started!

In this section I'm going to go over 11 different mindfulness exercises that will help to kick start your path towards a more mindful existence. You don't need to learn and perform all of these exercises. Just pick out the ones that you're most comfortable with and begin from there.

1. Mindful Breathing – I discussed this one in the chapter above under Breath Awareness meditation. You can practice this one for as little or as long as you'd like. I would start off small and try it for a couple of minutes. As you get more comfortable, begin to increase the amount of time. When I practice my breathing, I usually do so for about 20 minutes. However, if I need to center myself, I'll often take a few minutes out of my day to practice this exercise and get back on track.

2. Mindful Observation – In this exercise you can either sit or stand up. All you need to do is pick a object in your current environment and focus only on that object for one to two minutes. Don't do anything else put pay attention to the object you're looking at. Visually inspect every inch of the object and relax into harmony for as long a period as your concentration will allow you to.

3. Mindful Listening – This exercise is used to help open your ears to listening to sounds without judgment. A lot of the things we hear every day are influenced in some way by our prior experiences. Start this exercise by picking out a musical track you've never heard. Then close your eyes and put on a pair of headphones to block out all outside sound. Once you've begun listening to the track, try not to get drawn into any judgments of the music itself or the person singing it. Instead, let yourself follow the music thinking of nothing else.

4. Mindful Awareness - This exercise is meant to help you become more aware and find a deeper appreciation for even the simplest most mundane tasks. To begin this exercise, think of something that happens or that you do on a every day basis. Once you've thought of something, go ahead and do it, only this time take a moment to be mindful of where you are, how the thing you're doing benefits you, and how you are feeling in that precise moment.

5. Mindful Appreciation – Make a list of 5-10 things in your everyday life that normally go unnoticed or unappreciated. What these things are isn't important. It can be either people or objects. Once you've made your list start to give thanks and show some appreciation to them. The goal of this exercise is to begin noticing the things that go on in your life, that you normally take for granted, or let go unnoticed. Try to learn more about these things and appreciate how they benefit your life.

6. Mindful Immersion – The goal of this exercise is to learn how to be content in the given moment, instead of getting caught up in wanting and striving for other things all the time. For this exercise pick one of your normal tasks. Now, instead of doing it as quickly as possible, take the time to appreciate every aspect of the task while you're completing it. Don't think of finishing it. Immerse yourself in each action of the task. Feel and become the motions needed to complete the task. You want to align yourself mentally, spiritually, and physically so that you're fully in the moment enjoying each action you're taking.

7. Mindful Movement - This exercise involves you doing intentional movement like yoga, walking, or stretching. Your intention during this exercise is to focus on your body and breath, noticing any sensations when moving and any moments when you're still. This is one of my personal favorites as far as mindfulness exercises go.

8. Sitting Meditations – These can last for any period of time from only a few minutes to over an hour. There are countless variations you can practice but these types of meditations often involve using your breath as the main focus of the exercise. Some sitting meditations will also include awareness of your bodily sensations, sounds, feelings, and thoughts.

9. Body Scans – These exercises move your focus to attention around your body, showing curiosity in your experiences, while also observing every sensation as you gain awareness of it. You can find a variety of these different meditations for free online. They normally range between 3 minutes and an hour.

10. Guided Meditations - These are meditations that are led by other people. You can find a ton of these online for free or a nominal charge. They often come in a variety of easy to play formats. I suggest you should try as many as possible until you find the ones you're most comfortable with. In these meditations an expert will normally walk you through a set of mindfulness exercises and allow you to reach a deep meditative state.

11. Guided Imagery – This is a gentle yet profound exercise that directs and focuses your imagination in a more positive manner. These can be simple or very complex. It's often referred to as visualization, although this technique involves all of your senses and emotions. This form of meditation has been shown to have a positive effect on mental health and well being.

Chapter Four: Yoga & Mindfulness

In this chapter, you will learn:

- Yoga & Mindfulness

Yoga & Mindfulness

Many mindfulness practitioners find yoga and mindfulness to go hand in hand with one another. The poses used in yoga are great for helping to focus your mind and attention in a positive manner. At the same time yoga also allows you relieve tension and build physical strength.

Here is a good introductory to some of the poses you can use to help you focus and increase your mindfulness. While yoga may not be for everyone I urge you to give it a serious try. Not only is it good for your mind but it can work wonders on your physical health.

I've become incredibly flexible and limber over the last few years from practicing yoga. Old lingering injuries I used to have no longer bother me and I've got a lot more energy to get me through the day. Hopefully you'll see the benefits and incorporate it into your daily ritual.

Yoga Poses for Mindfulness

While I'm going to briefly discuss each of the poses I started off with when yoga training, I suggest going on a site like You Tube and finding videos of yoga routines and poses.

Personally, I've always been a visual learner, so I find seeing people perform the moves to be more helpful then reading descriptions of them. There's a ton of videos walking you through each step and showing you exactly where each part of your body should be during a particular pose. I'm in no way a professional yoga trainer so I'll try to explain each pose I use as best I can.

1. Corpse Pose

This is the initial pose that will start and end most sessions of yoga. All you need to do for this pose is lie down on your back, with your arms straight down by your sides, keeping your palms both turned upwards. Once you've done that move your feet about a foot or so apart from one another. Next, close your eyes and begin to practice breathing mindfully. Continue to do this until you've felt all the tension release itself from your body.

2. Downward Dog Pose

This is a popular move in yoga and is a little harder than say the cat or needle's eye poses. To perform this move get on your hands and knees. From there you should move your body so that the soles of both your feet are on the ground. You also want to lift your hips up, while straightening your legs, keeping both your arms out directly in front of you. You should be forming a triangle shape with your tailbone as the the top point of the triangle. Once you've gotten into this pose try taking at least 5-10 mindful breaths.

3. Cat Pose

For this pose get on your hands and knees, placing your hands underneath your shoulders and knees under your hips. Next, take a breath and gently curve your spine, tailbone, and neck making a C shape that's facing the floor. You want to allow your chin to tilt down towards your chest area.

Continue this pose for a few moments. Take a deep breath and alternate the pose. You'll want to pick up your head so it's going towards the sky and arch your spine downwards towards the floor so that your tailbone is sticking up in the air. Continue this pose for a few moments. Take a deep breath and alternate between poses a few more times.

4. Needle's Eye

From the corpse pose, bring your feet in close to your butt, while still keeping them about a hip's width apart. Then, press both the soles of your feet onto the ground.
First, pick up your right foot and pull your right foot in near to your chest area. Join both your hands around your right thigh area and keep stretching your muscles gently while your pulling the knee inwards.

If you're not that flexible don't worry you'll improve over time. After you've done the one leg, switch and do the same movement with the other one.

While you're performing these movements be sure to recognize how your body feels during the process. Make sure to keep taking mindful breaths throughout.

5. Warrior Pose

In a standing position, reach out both your arms to the sides, while moving both your feet so that they are wide apart from one another. Ideally your toes should be lining up under where your fingers are.

Next, turn your right foot so it's at a 90 degree angle, while turning your other foot slightly inwards. Don't lean, instead bend slightly so your right knee goes over your ankle. From here you need to stretch both your arms as far as you can and continue to hold the pose as long as you're able. Don't forget to breath.

Switch sides and repeat the process. Don't be alarmed if you have difficulty with this one at first. It's more difficult than the other poses mentioned. It will take some time before you get the hang of it and build up your endurance.

6. Fish Lord Pose

For this pose you need to sit down on the ground cross legged. You'll need to place your left foot up and then underneath your right thigh area. When you've done that you're left heel should also be next to your right side hip.

Cross your right leg over top your left leg, while pressing the sole of your foot into the ground right next to your left thigh area. Using your left hand, hold onto your right knee, then twist your spine so you'll be able to actually reach your right hand behind yourself.

Stretch the top of your head towards the sky and remember to breath and stay in the moment. Continue to hold this pose as long as you're able to. Once you're done, switch and repeat the process on the other side.

7. Bend Forward

Finish off by relaxing all your muscles from your last pose and stretch both your legs out directly in front of you with both feet together. Push your legs into the ground, feeling the rush of energy come flowing over your muscles. Flex all your toes forward in an upwards direction, lifting your chest towards the ceiling. Continue to breathe like this a few times.

Next, you want to bend over and reach towards your feet, or as far as you can reach. Try rotating your thighs, so you'll be able to lie over them, with your chest area bent over top your knees. Slowly breathe in and out a few times. Hold this pose as long as you can manage and then release. Go back into corpse pose and take a few last deep breaths.

That's it you're all done. Feel free to continue with more advanced exercises or move on to your preferred form of meditation. Don't worry if you're not able to perform these poses or hold them for long when you're new. It takes time to strengthen these muscles and your flexibility. Over time it will get easier, and you'll find yourself holding each pose for longer periods of time.

Chapter Five: Meditation & Mindfulness

In this chapter, you will learn:

- Meditation & Mindfulness

- Mindfulness Meditation Instruction

Meditation & Mindfulness

In this section I'm going to discuss the important role mediation plays in attaining mindfulness. Before I started trying to become more mindful I never tried or gave much thought to meditation. I actually kinda looked down on it. I thought it was nonsense. I'm not really sure where my negative thoughts came from on the subject, since I really knew very little about it. I admit, it was something I needed to work through when I first started out.

It took some time and convincing from friends, but I eventually realized the positive affects meditation could have on my life. After a few months of practice, I was blown away at what a difference it made in how I not only viewed the world around me, but how I felt inside about myself. Now I meditate daily in the morning, and go on frequent walking meditations during the course of my week. Hopefully you'll gain some of the same benefits I did from embracing the power of meditation.

While some people learn how to meditate to enhance and deepen their spiritual growth, others practice outside its religious setting for health and wellness purposes. I fell into this category, as I'm sure many of you will as well.

I've found meditation can be used to manage stress and alleviate a lot of the pressure we tend to put on ourselves. Meditation teaches the mind how to be still and behave. It allows us to quiet the chatter in our minds and turn off the self internalized monologue that constantly interferes with our inner peace.

By practicing mindfulness meditation daily, you'll begin to train your mind to find calm, appreciation, happiness and love in everyday interactions and circumstances. It will allow you to push past obstacles that once seemed insurmountable, while giving you a greater sense of purpose and sense of well being.

When being mindful is the main tool in our meditation, we must be aware of our breath (or whatever we're using as the primary focus of our meditation), so that it can be properly used to include all of our mental and physical processes. This way, over time we can start to become more and more mindful of all our actions and thoughts.

People often think that when we meditate we're trying to stop every thought and let our minds rest in peace with the complete absence of thought. New practitioners biggest complaint is that they often feel they're doing something wrong because they aren't able to turn off their thoughts. However, thinking that is the meaning of meditation is incorrect. You're supposed to have thoughts when you meditate.

Mindfulness meditation is what we do with thoughts when they occur. When you feel like you're being distracted by your thoughts, you'll want to bring back all your attention to whatever the object of your meditation is. That's how you learn how to relate differently to any future distractions. Over time it will dramatically improve your ability to both focus and concentrate.

Meditation comes in many forms. I suggest finding a local teacher or group to help you out when first getting started. Some places these might be available are at local gyms, yoga centers, houses of worship and senior centers. You can also ask your doctor for recommendations. Personally, I had a local yoga center with a great teacher so I didn't need to search for long before I found someone to guide me.

Mindfulness Mediation Instruction

In this section I'll go over a few simple instructions on how you can get started with mindfulness meditation. You can use any form of meditation you prefer but this is my personal favorite and is the one I practice most often.

Start by either getting a chair to sit in or a cushion to sit on the floor with. Always keep your spine straight. Slowly relax into a comfortable sitting posture. Begin by taking a few deep and calming breaths. You want to allow your body and mind to get completely relaxed, while at the same time making sure your mind stays alert and attentive to the moment. Take note of any areas in your body that are feeling tense and any areas that are feeling relaxed. Don't attempt to force or fix anything. Just let your body go with the flow.

Try and remember to allow your mind to remain soft. You want to allow your awareness to wash over your entire body. Continue to feel the sensation of sitting. Use your mind to help you sidestep any natural tendencies to think about your body or imagine it's existence. You want to to let images and thoughts come and go as they do without feeling bothered or concerned by them.

Continue to feel all of your body and any awareness that comes from within you, but not from your mind. Being aware of your body will help to anchor you and focus your attention on the present moment.

Now begin to sweep all of that awareness through the rest of your body. Be sure to feel every sensation. Don't attach any goals or agendas just focus on the moment. Stay mindful of all these new sensations and stay in the moment.

Once some time has elapsed, you can begin to move your awareness to any sounds around you. Awareness of sound will help you to create openness, receptivity and spaciousness in your mind. Try and stay aware of of not only the sounds but of the silence that occurs in-between those sounds. As you did with the sensations of your body, you'll want to shift your awareness away from trying to define the sounds, or having thoughts regarding the sounds. The only thing you want to do is try and hear the sound exactly as it is.

After some time has passed, you can begin to bring back your full attention to your breathing. Be sure to locate your breath where it's clearest and keep your awareness there. For me this is often the sensation I get from the rising and falling of my chest.

When breathing, let your breath go naturally without trying to control it in any fashion. Feel your breath only from within your breath itself, not from your head. You want to feel the full cycle of your breath from the very beginning to the very end.

When doing this, let go of anything around you. Let it all rest in the background. You want your breathing to be natural without you trying to force it. Your goal is to rest in a state of deep relaxation, being mindful of your surroundings and the sensation of your breathing.

As your mind begins to wander, be aware and guide yourself back to your anchor without any judgment. Once you've had some practice, you'll notice it becomes like second nature to do this. At first, I had hard time not negatively judging myself for wandering off. I was able to work through those feelings and stop judging myself over time.

Keep yourself in the moment, being mindful of your surroundings for as long as you're able to at first. Just focus on each breath, keeping yourself anchored. I started out just doing a few minutes a day and worked my way up slowly over time. Now I can meditate for long periods of time if I so desire.

I've found the more I meditate, the more I'm able to get rid of any fears and unnecessary attachments. It allows me to live a more joyful life, filled with wisdom and compassion.

Chapter Six: Anxiety & Mindfulness

In this chapter, you will learn:

- Anxiety & Mindfulness

Anxiety & Mindfulness

Many people suffering from anxiety have found that meditation and being more mindful in their every day lives can make a huge impact. It's been shown that mindfulness can drastically reduce the amount of stress and anxiety in a person's life. By being more aware of ourselves moment to moment we're able to rewire our brains to deal with stress and other anxiety triggers in a healthier way.

Relaxation and anxiety are polar opposite states of being. If you're experiencing one then you won't be experiencing the other. That's the reason why being mindful is a great antidote to any stress and anxiety you may be dealing with. Stress and anxiety aren't able to burden our minds if we don't let the negative thoughts into our minds.

Mindfulness teaches us to live in the moment, while focusing on what we are currently doing. It teaches us how to regain our focus when our mind begins to inevitably wander off. By focusing on the moment and the sensations of our body it makes it more difficult to consciously worry.

It takes some time and practice to learn the techniques needed to quiet down your mind. Also, it won't miraculously cure all your anxiety issues, but it can help to ease them quite a bit. In this section I'm going to go over a few of the ways I like to practice mindfulness, especially when dealing with anxiety issues.

1. Come Back – When you feel like things are starting to go off the rails, take the opportunity to stop for a moment and tell yourself to "come back." What I mean by this is that you want to take a few mindful breaths and focus only what you're doing in that given moment. Don't let any outside thoughts take you away from what you're doing in the present.

2. Body Scan – There are lots of great scripts for different body scans available for free online. In essence you just want to meditate by focusing on what sensations are going on in your body at that precise moment.

3. Three Senses – With this technique you experience the current moment using your sense of sight, touch, and sound. Begin by taking a few deep breaths. Then ask yourself these questions:

Name three things I can hear (ex. the TV, the radio, other people talking)

Name three things I can see (ex. the sky, the furniture, my pets)

Name three things I can touch (ex. the floor, my clothing, the glasses on my face).

Answer each of these questions to yourself, taking time to answer each one. This will force you to focus on the current moment rather than any negative thoughts you may be having.

4. Mindfulness Tasks or Cooking – When I've had a tough day I like to come home and cook a nice healthy meal. However, while I'm cooking I make it a point to really be mindful of each step I'm taking and really experience creating the meal. I carry this over to eating the meal as well, trying to enjoy and experience each and every bite of my food. I find that once I've finished cooking, eating and cleaning up, all while practicing mindfulness, whatever issues I was having during the day that was raising my anxiety levels have melted away, leaving me relaxed and ready to enjoy the rest of my evening. These same principles will work when applied to most normal daily tasks and chores.

5. Mindfulness Walking – If something gets me stressed out at work I like to take a break and go on a quick walk. I use this time to practice my mindfulness, letting whatever issues got me worked up fade into the background. By taking a break from the stressful activity, focusing only on the moment, I'm allowing my mind and body a chance to calm down and get over whatever issue had me riled up in the first place. Once I'm done, I find I usually have a much clearer mind and I'm ready to find tackle whatever obstacle I need to face head on.

6. Guided Meditations – I find one of the times my anxiety levels are at their highest is when I'm trying to go to sleep. I used to have issues with my mind not wanting to turn off and constantly chattering away with negative thoughts. In order to gain control over your mind you need to train it to quiet down when you want it to. I've found that listening to guided meditations before sleep that specifically deal with lessening stress and anxiety have worked wonders in getting me to a point where I can close my eyes for bed without worrying about having an anxiety attack. Once you learn to slow down and soothe your mind you'll find that most bouts of anxiety can be dealt with before they spiral out of control.

Remember, you aren't your anxiety. Stress and anxiety aren't a permanent part of who you are as a person. They are just negative thoughts and feelings. Don't try and fight your anxiety, just take it in for what it is, knowing that it will pass, and you are the only one in that is in control of your mind.

I suggest also trying to learn from your anxiety. Oftentimes our fears and anxiety uncover areas of our life that need some attention. By stepping back and evaluating what your anxiety is trying to tell you, you'll be able to figure out what actions are needed to solve some of the problems you're dealing with, perhaps putting those fears to rest once and for all.

Chapter Seven: 55+ Mindfulness Tips for Beginner's

In this chapter, you will learn:

- 55+ Mindfulness Tips for Beginner's

55+ Mindfulness Tips

In this section I'll go over 55+ tips that will help you become more mindful over yourself and your surroundings. I have this list in a file on my computer that I can reference whenever I feel the need to refocus. I hope these tips have the same positive on impact on your life that they did in mine.

1. Whenever you need to relax, simply concentrate only on your breathing and allow your subconscious to take over.

2. When driving, turn off all music or talk radio, experiencing the sound of silence. It takes a bit to get used to. You'll feel like something may be missing. However, after time you'll see that with silence you're able to otherwise fill your mind with different perceptions, many of which are very rewarding. Practicing this can leave your mind calmer, quieter and much more focused overall.

3. Eat slower than normal. Try eating a meal in silence each week as an experiment. This will help you experience the eating more fully. You may also want to cut out reading, listening to music, or watching TV while you're eating. Eliminating these things will allow you to become more attuned with how you eat and will give you more awareness when you're eating among other people.

4. When you're working, use your breaks to really relax instead of just pausing on what you're doing. For example, instead of having a drink and talking with your fellow workers, take a short walk and meditate.

5. Be aware of how often you're letting your mind dwell on past memories or future possibilities. Is this something that is necessary? Are these memories affecting you negatively? The future and the past are places we visit for planning and learning. However, many of us end up living in the past or future, instead of focusing on the here and now. Don't let yourself fall into that trap.

6. Use your environmental cues as a reminder to continually center yourself. Allow the cues around you to help signal to yourself that it's time you take a minute to pause, take a deep breath, and become more aware of your bodily sensation. When you do this it allows your mind to settle down and regroup.

7. When going to work and stopped at a light, take a moment to pay close attention to what's around you, where your mind is at, and your breathing.

8. When your done with your work day and you're walking to your vehicle, focus on your breathing and the air around you. Listen to any sounds you hear. Your goal is to be able to walk without the feeling of being rushed. You shouldn't feel anxious to get home.

9. When you get home after work, be sure to say hello to everyone in your home. Look into each of their eyes when doing this. Afterwards, take about 5-15 minutes to stay quiet and still. If you happen to live by yourself, enter your home and embrace the quietness of your environment and the feeling of that silence.

10. Spend some more time in nature. I take long walks and hikes whenever possible.

11. Notice how your mind is constantly judging things. Don't take these judgements too seriously. These thoughts aren't who you are.

12. Practice listening without judging. It's harder to do than it sounds.

13. Don't feel forced to always be doing something. If you have some free time take that time to simply be.

14. When walking, be aware of how your weight is shifting, the sensations you feel in your feet. Focus more on yourself and less on where you're headed.

15. Take some time to focus only on your breathing. Feel the flow of your breath and how your chest rises and falls.

16. Take notice of what you're doing while you're doing it. Try and be in tune with all your senses.

17. When you're eating, notice the texture and colors of your food as well as how it tastes.

18. If your mind begins to wander to negative thinking, bring it back gently to your breath.

19. Remember your thoughts are only thoughts, You aren't obligated to react to them or even believe them.

20. Think of all the activities you do that you tend to zone out in. Some examples are texting, doing chores, web surfing, & driving. Take some time and practice being more aware when participating in these activities.

21. Practice short bursts of mindfulness. Our brains react better to shorter sessions of mindfulness many times throughout the day, rather than a few long sessions of being mindful.

22. Pick out a prompt to help you remember to be mindful. It could be getting a cup of coffee triggers you to take some time to be mindful, or hanging your coat up when you get home from work. Whatever triggers help you remember to practice mindfulness on daily basis will work just fine.

23. Learn to properly meditate. Mindfulness is a skill we need to learn and sharpen over time. Being able to meditate properly will allow you to accomplish this.

24. Practice being mindful while you're waiting. Whether it's in line or at a doctor's appointment, these moments are great opportunities to practice being more mindful.

25. Practice first thing when you wake up in the morning. I find this helps me set the tone for the rest of my day and gets my body more in tune with my surroundings. Take a few minutes before you start reading your paper, watching TV, or getting ready for whatever tasks you have on hand that day.

26. Right after waking up, before getting out of your bed, focus on your breathing. Observe at least 5 mindful breaths.

27. Be aware of changes in posture. You need to stay aware of how your mind and body feel when you're going from lying down, up to sitting, up to standing, up to walking. Notice your posture from one transition to the next.

28. Use any sound you hear as a bell for mindfulness. Really use that opportunity to listen and be present.

29. During the course of your day, take a moment from time to time to focus on your breathing. Observe 5 mindful breaths.

30. Pay attention when you're eating. Consciously consume your food, bringing awareness to tasting, chewing, and swallowing. Realize that your food was connected to something that helped nourished its growth.

31. Bring awareness to talking and listening. Can you listen to someone without either agreeing or disagreeing, disliking or liking, or planning what things you'll say when it's your turn to talk? While talking, can you simply state what you need to say without understating or overstating? Are you able to notice how both your body and mind feel? The more you practice being aware and present the easier it'll get over time.

32. Focus some more attention on your normal everyday activities. These include washing, brushing your teeth, and getting dressed. Try and practice bringing mindfulness to each of these activities.

33. Notice any points on your body where you're feeling tight. Try and breathe into them, while exhaling let go of any excess tension you feel. Do you have tension stored in any part of your body. For example, your shoulders, neck, jaw, stomach or back? If so, try stretching and practicing yoga at least once each day.

34. Before bed, take a moment to bring some attention to your breathing. The same as you did when you wake up in the morning. Observe 5 mindful breaths.

35. Create a 15 minute invite on your calendar regarding mindfulness for each day and be sure to commit to always spending that time with yourself.

36. Take breaks from your job to help gain perspective on what you're doing.

37. Find some other people at your job who are interested in becoming more mindful and practice your mindfulness together.

38. Find a mindfulness mentor. This can be anyone practicing that you can get advice from and can talk about your practicing with.

39. Focus on individual tasks instead of trying to multitask.

40. Try and take a walk outside every day leaving your phone behind or turned off.

41. Try riding a bike to work. You'll need to be mindful if you're biking through some traffic.

42. Pause and center yourself for about 30 seconds at your job before diving into the work you have to accomplish.

43. Turn a unused closet or room into a meditation space.

44. Implement boundaries to help let your mind shut off. For instance turn off your phone after 9 pm or don't bring it in your bedroom before going to sleep.

45. Don't beat yourself up if you get distracted. There will be days that are far more hectic than others.

46. They call it "practice" for a good reason – It takes a lot of repetition to properly develop your mindfulness muscle.

47. Not everyone will develop there mindfulness habits at the same pace. For some it may take as little as 8 weeks. For others it will take longer. Just keep going and you'll get there eventually.

48. Don't get dragged down by your problems. Problems can be an opportunity to grow. Learn to recognize problems and solve them.

49. Don't wallow in your past. Live each day without regret. The more you look to the past the harder it will be to enjoy your time in the present.

50. Always create new goals for yourself. Give yourself something to look forward to each day.

51. Take time to appreciate yourself. If you can't learn to find value in yourself you'll have a hard time finding it in others.

52. Learn something new everyday. Even if it's something small. Continued growth and knowledge will only benefit you in the long run. Making mistakes is par for the course. It's only that we learn from our mistakes that matters.

53. Appreciate the small things your friends and family do for you. Do small things for the people in your life to show how much you care.

54. Mindfulness is not something to do a few minutes a day. Over time it should become a part of your life. The goal is to bring more awareness and compassion to every situation you find yourself in. Learning how to be more mindful in all situations will only benefit you long term.

55. Try out aromatherapy to increase your focus. I've found that smell helps me focus more than chants or mantras. Most people don't think to try aromatherapy. I know I didn't at first.

56. Have an open and clean space to meditate in. You want as little distraction surrounding you as possible when meditating. This especially rings true when you're first starting out. Try to find an area that is free of clutter and distraction when meditating at home.

57. Let in some air and natural light to your meditation area. Many people, myself included, are able to focus much better when breathing in fresh air and surrounded by sunlight.

58. Choose the kind of meditation that resonates with you. Don't practice a form of mediation just because it's what someone said you should do. Learn the different methods, and decide for yourself. The more comfortable you are, the better chance you'll have at sticking with it. While I enjoy mindfulness meditation and walking meditations, my partner prefers yoga and guided sitting meditations.

Chapter Eight: 15 Mindfulness Apps & Resources to Improve Your Life

In this chapter, you will learn:

- 15 Mindfulness Apps & Resources to Improve Your Life

15 Mindfulness Apps & Resources to Improve Your Life

In this section I'll discuss and share with you 15 different mindfulness apps & resources you can use in your every day life. Not all of these will apply to everyone. Feel free to pick and choose the ones that best work for your particular situation. Many of these have made a real difference in my life and I highly recommend them.

<u>1. Stop, Breathe & Think App</u>

This app is available on the Android, iPhone and the Web. This app gives a good variety of basic meditations, that will range in lengths. Some things included are mindfulness meditation, body scan practice, and loving-kindness meditation. This app is ideal for both the home and when you're on the go. This app does a good job of harnessing the emotional components by having you tell it how you feel both physically and mentally.

From there it will then give you some suggestions on different meditations to practice in order to get the most out of your session. This is a free app although there are special features you can unlock for a small fee. This is the main app I use on a daily basis.

2. Buddhify

This app is available on both Android and iPhone. This app comes with over 80 different guided meditations you can use depending on your schedule and where you're at emotionally. In all there's over 11 hours worth of meditations. This is a paid app and has a one time fee of $2.99.

3. The Mindfulness Training App

This app is available on the iPhone. This app will give you a small taste of the teachings of many of the main figures in mindfulness. These figures include Jack Kornfield, Jon Kabat-Zinn, and Tara Brach. If you're a newbie when it comes to the world of meditation, this application is an excellent way to gain a deeper understanding of what mindfulness is all about.

This app also contains plenty of discussions involving advanced insights for more seasoned mindfulness practitioners. My main issue with this app is that it's a bit clunky to navigate at times and is only available on the iPhone. Otherwise this is one of my favorite apps to recommend to others. This app is free to download but has many different in app purchases to choose from.

4. Insight Timer

This app is available on both the Android and iPhone. This app is a mediation timer which also functions as a guide to mindfulness. People using the app can share all their mediation times with other users and friends. They can also check in on different people meditating in their area. This app also comes with guided meditations from teachers like Jack Kornfield, Sharon Salzberg and Elisha Goldstein. Finally this app also comes with a timer that will allow you to keep time of your mediation. This app is free to download but does have in app purchases of $4.99. Definitely worth your time to check out! This one is a favorite of many of my friends.

5. Headspace

This app is available on Android, iPhone, and the Web. This app is like a trainer for the mind. With tons of content including different series focused on health, relationships, and performance. This is a paid monthly app that comes with a 10 day free trial where they go over 10 different practices to help you get started. I'd recommend trying this out on the trial and seeing how you like it before making any longer commitments. I use this app and enjoy it but having to pay a monthly fee isn't for everyone.

6. Calm

This app is available on Android, iPhone, and the Web. This is a free app that allows you to choose both sounds and background scenery. For example, a sunny seaside with the sounds of crashing waves. After you've chosen your selections you can then set a timer and relax for the amount of time you designated. Personally, I use this app before bed to help put me in a relaxed state.

7. Mindfulness Meditation Mental Workout

This app is available on Android, iPhone and the Web. This app is designed by meditation expert Stephan Bodian. It comes in either a free lite version or the full paid version ($12.99 / 1 year). With this app you'll get guided meditations, relaxation exercises, body scans, inspirational talks, meditation instructions and a 8 week plan filled with daily activities to help you put what you've learned into practice. I've only tried the lite version of this app as I already use many other mindfulness tools, however I've gotten really good feedback from a few of my friends who've purchased it.

8. *Mindful*

This is a website devoted to mindfulness. It's home to it's own magazine and newsletter on mindfulness. This site contains lots of great articles discussing mindfulness, and how we can use it to positively impact our daily lives. I'm constantly learning new things from the articles on this site and it's a wonderful source on all the latest new resources and tools to try out.

9. *Relax Melodies*

This app is available on both Android & iPhone. This app contains more than just melodies. It also has beautiful natural scenery to choose from and a selection of meditations. This is a free app and one I definitely recommend trying out.

10. *Meditation Timer Pro*

This app is available on the iPhone. This app is simple to use and navigate. It offers prepare time, interval time and cool down time. It also offers a variety of sounds and background images. My favorite feature is that it will save logs of your meditations and keep statistics on your progress. You can also set reminders to let you know when it's time to mediate. This is a free app and one I would use all the time if not for the fact that I recently switched to an Android based phone.

11. Take A Break

This app is available on both Android & iPhone. This app is great for when you need a reminder to take a short 7 minute break for relaxation or a longer 13 minute long break for meditation. Comes with a variety of calming sounds and music. This is a free app that is good for people who get wrapped up in work and forget to take some time out to relax and meditate during the day.

12. Omvana

This app is available on Android, iPhone, and the Web. This app offers over 500 of the world's top audio's on meditation, body, mind, productivity, lifestyle and relationships. It comes with guided meditations from famous authors and a variety of inspirational tracks to help you get inspired each day. This app is free to download and then has in app purchases ranging from .99 cents to $7.99. This is an app worth checking out and offers a ton of content.

13. Walking Meditations

This app is available on both Android & iPhone. This app is perfect for anyone that has trouble sitting still when wanting to meditate. This app helps bring your meditation into each moment of your day. This app will guide you to experience both your body and your surroundings fully as you take a walk, letting go of any preoccupations that normally inhabit your mind. I really enjoyed what this app taught me. When I first started out I had a real problem with remaining still. This app helped me mediate on the move until I learned to slow down. This app costs $1.99 to purchase.

14. American Mindfulness Research Association (AMRA)

This website is the home to AMRA. Here you can find mindfulness health articles, mindfulness measurement tools, along with mindfulness research and training programs located across the globe.

15. Mindful Net

This website is dedicated to mindfulness and providing access to as much content on the subject as possible. Has links to research, articles, resources, apps. and other sites that can help you learn more about mindfulness.

Here is a short list of mindfulness books I've read over the years and found to be very helpful:

The Miracle of Mindfulness: An Introduction to the Practice of Meditation by Thich Nhat Hanh

Being Good: Buddhist Ethics for Everyday Life by Hsing Yun

The Art of Living: Vipassana Meditation as Taught by S. N. Goenka by William Hart

Bonus Chapter: 200+ Mindfulness Quotes to Live Your Life By!

In this chapter, you will learn:

- 200+ Mindfulness Quotes to Live Your Life By!

200+ Mindfulness Quotes to Live Your Life By!

In this section I'll go over 200+ quotes relating to mindfulness that I've come across over the years. Whenever I'm feeling stressed or out of sync, I like to read over these quotes. They always leave me feeling inspired, ready to take control of my life. Hopefully you enjoy these quotes as much as I do.

1. "Do every act of your life as though it were the last act of your life." - Marcus Aurelius

2. "Keep your eyes on the stars and your feet on the ground." – Theodore Roosevelt

3. "The present moment is filled with joy and happiness. If you are attentive, you will see it." - Thich Nhat Hanh

4. "Ever tried. Ever failed. No matter. Try again. Fail again. Fail better." -Anonymous

5. "Looking at beauty in the world, is the first step to purifying the mind." - Amit Ray

6. "The secret of getting ahead is getting started." - Mark Twain

7. "Expect the problems and eat them for breakfast." - Alfred A. Montapert

8. "Be kind whenever possible. It is always possible." - Dalai Lama

9. "Paradise is not a place it's a state of consciousness." - Sri Chinmoy

10. "Drink your tea slowly and reverently, as if it is the axis on which the world earth revolves – slowly, evenly, without rushing toward the future; live the actual moment. Only this moment is life." – Thich Nhat Hanh

11. "Mindfulness is the aware, balanced acceptance of the present experience. It isn't more complicated than that. It is opening to or receiving the present moment, pleasant or unpleasant, just as it is, without either clinging to it or rejecting it." – Sylvia Boorstein

12. "Perhaps ultimately, spiritual simply means experiencing wholeness and interconnectedness directly, a seeing that individuality and the totality are interwoven, that nothing is separate or extraneous. If you see in this way, then everything becomes spiritual in its deepest sense. Doing science is spiritual. So is washing the dishes." – Jon Kabat-Zinn

13. "Between stimulus and response there is a space. In that space is our power to choose our response. In our response lies our growth and our freedom." – Victor Frankl

14. "Mindfulness is about being fully awake in our lives. It is about perceiving the exquisite vividness of each moment. We also gain immediate access to our own powerful inner resources for insight, transformation, and healing." – Jon Kabat-Zinn

15. "There are only two ways to live your life. One is as though nothing is a miracle. The other is as though everything is a miracle." – Albert Einstein

16. "You have a treasure within you that is infinitely greater than anything the world can offer." – Eckhart Tolle

17. "Wanting to reform the world without discovering one's true self is like trying to cover the world with leather to avoid the pain of walking on stones and thorns. It is much simpler to wear shoes." – Sri Ramana Maharshi

18. "To see a world in a grain of sand and heaven in a wild flower, Hold infinity in the palm of your hand and eternity in an hour." – William Blake

19. "If you clean the floor with love, you have given the world an invisible painting." – Osho

20. "The most fundamental aggression to ourselves, the most fundamental harm we can do to ourselves, is to remain ignorant by not having the courage and the respect to look at ourselves honestly and gently." – Pema Chodran

21. "Happiness is your nature. It is not wrong to desire it. What is wrong is seeking it outside when it is inside." – Sri Ramana Maharshi

22. "Mindfulness is simply being aware of what is happening right now without wishing it were different; enjoying the pleasant without holding on when it changes (which it will); being with the unpleasant without fearing it will always be this way (which it won't)." – James Baraz

23. "Your vision will become clear only when you look into your heart. Who looks outside, dreams. Who looks inside, awakens." – Carl Jung

24. "The moment one gives close attention to anything, even a blade of grass, it becomes a mysterious, awesome, indescribably magnificent world in itself." – Henry Miller

25. "When you realize nothing is lacking, the whole world belongs to you." - Lao Tzu

26. "As soon as we wish to be happier, we are no longer happy." - Walter Landor

27. "The best way to capture moments is to pay attention. This is how we cultivate mindfulness. Mindfulness means being awake. It means knowing what you are doing." - Jon Kabat-Zinn

28. "If you want others to be happy, practice compassion. If you want to be happy, practice compassion." - Dalai Lama

29. "In today's rush, we all think too much — seek too much — want too much — and forget about the joy of just being." - Eckhart Tolle

30. "If we learn to open our hearts, anyone, including the people who drive us crazy, can be our teacher." - Pema Chodron

31. "If the doors of perception were cleansed, everything would appear to man as it is, infinite." - William Blake

32. "Suffering usually relates to wanting things to be different than they are." - Allan Lokos

33. "In the end, just three things matter: How well we have lived. How well we have loved. How well we have learned to let go" - Jack Kornfield

34. "Everything is created twice, first in the mind and then in reality." - Robin S. Sharma

35. "Don't believe everything you think. Thoughts are just that – thoughts." - Allan Lokos
36. "In this moment, there is plenty of time. In this moment, you are precisely as you should be. In this moment, there is infinite possibility." - Victoria Moran

37. "Mindfulness isn't difficult, we just need to remember to do it." - Sharon Salzberg

38. "Respond; don't react. Listen; don't talk. Think; don't assume." - Raji Lukkoor

39. "Each morning we are born again. What we do today is what matters most." - Buddha

40. "If you concentrate on finding whatever is good in every situation, you will discover that your life will suddenly be filled with gratitude, a feeling that nurtures the soul." - Rabbi Harold Kushner

41. "I wish that life should not be cheap, but sacred. I wish the days to be as centuries, loaded, fragrant." - Ralph Waldo Emerson

42. "Begin at once to live, and count each separate day as a separate life." - Seneca

43. "It's only when we truly know and understand that we have a limited time on earth – and that we have no way of knowing when our time is up – that we will begin to live each day to the fullest, as if it was the only one we had." - Elisabeth Kübler-Ross

44. "There's only one reason why you're not experiencing bliss at this present moment, and it's because you're thinking or focusing on what you don't have.... But, right now you have everything you need to be in bliss." - Anthony de Mello

45. "Observe the space between your thoughts, then observe the observer." - Hamilton Boudreaux

46. "Our own worst enemy cannot harm us as much as our unwise thoughts. No one can help us as much as our own compassionate thoughts." - Buddha

47. "The mind in its natural state can be compared to the sky, covered by layers of cloud which hide its true nature." - Kalu Rinpoche

48. "The basic root of happiness lies in our minds; outer circumstances are nothing more than adverse or favorable." - Matthieu Ricard

49. "Impermanence is a principle of harmony. When we don't struggle against it, we are in harmony with reality." - Pema Chodron

50. "If one were truly aware of the value of human life, to waste it blithely on distractions and the pursuit of vulgar ambitions would be the height of confusion." - Dilgo Khyentse Rinpoche

51. "We are awakened to the profound realization that the true path to liberation is to let go of everything." - Jack Kornfield

52. "Knowledge does not mean mastering a great quantity of different information, but understanding the nature of mind. This knowledge can penetrate each one of our thoughts and illuminate each one of our perceptions." - Matthieu Ricard

53. "To diminish the suffering of pain, we need to make a crucial distinction between the pain of pain, and the pain we create by our thoughts about the pain. Fear, anger, guilt, loneliness and helplessness are all mental and emotional responses that can intensify pain." - Howard Cutler

54. "Why, if we are as pragmatic as we claim, don't we begin to ask ourselves seriously: Where does our real future lie?" - Sogyal Rinpoche

55. "We have only now, only this single eternal moment opening and unfolding before us, day and night." - Jack Kornfield

56. "Mindful and creative, a child who has neither a past, nor examples to follow, nor value judgements, simply lives, speaks and plays in freedom." - Arnaud Desjardins

57. "Feelings come and go like clouds in a windy sky. Conscious breathing is my anchor." – Thich Nhat Hanh

58. "If you want to conquer the anxiety of life, live in the moment, live in the breath." – Amit Ray

59. "If someone comes along and shoots an arrow into your heart, it's fruitless to stand there and yell at the person. It would be much better to turn your attention to the fact that there's an arrow in your heart..." — Pema Chödrön

60. "Feelings, whether of compassion or irritation, should be welcomed, recognized, and treated on an absolutely equal basis; because both are ourselves. The tangerine I am eating is me. The mustard greens I am planting are me. I plant with all my heart and mind. I clean this teapot with the kind of attention I would have were I giving the baby Buddha or Jesus a bath. Nothing should be treated more carefully than anything else. In mindfulness, compassion, irritation, mustard green plant, and teapot are all sacred." — Thich Nhat Hanh

61. "Do not ruin today with mourning tomorrow." — Catherynne M. Valente

62. "Few of us ever live in the present. We are forever anticipating what is to come or remembering what has gone." — Louis L'Amour

63. "Be happy in the moment, that's enough. Each moment is all we need, not more." — Mother Teresa

64. "In this moment, there is plenty of time. In this moment, you are precisely as you should be. In this moment, there is infinite possibility." — Victoria Moran

65. "I don't need anyone else to distract me from myself anymore, like I always thought I would." — Charlotte Eriksson

66. "Mind is a flexible mirror, adjust it, to see a better world." — Amit Ray

67. "Life is a dance. Mindfulness is witnessing that dance." — Amit Ray

68. "Restore your attention or bring it to a new level by dramatically slowing down whatever you're doing." — Sharon Salzberg

69. "One is a great deal less anxious if one feels perfectly free to be anxious, and the same may be said of guilt." – Alan W. Watts

70. "Respond; don't react. Listen; don't talk. Think; don't assume." – Raji Lukkoor

71. "Don't let a day go by without asking who you are...each time you let a new ingredient to enter your awareness." – Deepak Chopra

72. "In a true you-and-I relationship, we are present mindfully, non intrusively, the way we are present with things in nature. We do not tell a birch tree it should be more like an elm. We face it with no agenda, only an appreciation that becomes participation: 'I love looking at this birch' becomes 'I am this birch' and then 'I and this birch are opening to a mystery that transcends and holds us both." – David Richo

73. "If you're reading these words, perhaps it's because something has kicked open the door for you, and you're ready to embrace change. It isn't enough to appreciate change from afar, or only in the abstract, or as something that can happen to other people but not to you. We need to create change for ourselves, in a workable way, as part of our everyday lives." – Sharon Salzberg

74. "It stands to reason that anyone who learns to live well will die well. The skills are the same: being present in the moment, and humble, and brave, and keeping a sense of humor." – Victoria Moran

75. "You have to remember one life, one death—this one! To enter fully the day, the hour, the moment whether it appears as life or death, whether we catch it on the in breath or out breath, requires only a moment, this moment. And along with it all the mindfulness we can muster, and each stage of our ongoing birth, and the confident joy of our inherent luminosity." – Stephen Levine

76. "Whatever you eye falls on - for it will fall on what you love - will lead you to the questions of your life, the questions that are incumbent upon you to answer, because that is how the mind works in concert with the eye. The things of this world draw us where we need to go." — Mary Rose O'Reilley

77. "Treat everyone you meet as if they were you." — Doug Dillon

78. "Most of us take for granted that time flies, meaning that it passes too quickly. But in the mindful state, time doesn't really pass at all. There is only a single instant of time that keeps renewing itself over and over with infinite variety." — Deepak Chopra

79. "It's good to have an end in mind but in the end what counts is how you travel." — Orna Ross

80. Through recognizing and realizing the empty essence, instead of being selfish and self-centered, one feels very open and free" — Tsoknyi Rinpoche

81. "Learn to say no to demands, requests, invitations, and activities that leave you with no time for yourself. Until I learned to say no, and mean it, I was always overloaded by stress. You may feel guilty and selfish at first for guarding your down- time, but you'll soon find that you are a much nicer, more present, more productive person in each instance you do choose to say yes." — Holly Mosier

82. "The mind which is created quick to love, is responsive to everything that is pleasing, soon as by pleasure it is awakened into activity. Your apprehensive faculty draws an impression from a real object, and unfolds it within you, so that it makes the mind turn thereto. And if, being turned, it inclines towards it, that inclination is love; that is nature, which through pleasure is bound anew within you." — Dante Alighieri

83. "Walk as if you are kissing the Earth with your feet." — Thich Nhat Hanh

84. "A mind set in its ways is wasted. Don't do it." — Eric Schmidt

85. "All beings want to be happy, yet so very few know how. It is out of ignorance that any of us cause suffering, for ourselves or for others" — Sharon Salzberg

86. "Our culture encourages us to plan every moment and fill our schedules with one activity and obligation after the next, with no time to just be. But the human body and mind require downtime to rejuvenate. I have found my greatest moments of joy and peace just sitting in silence, and then I take that joy and peace with me out into the world." — Holly Mosier

87. "Mindfulness has never met a cognition it didn't like." — Daniel J. Siegel

88. "Like a child standing in a beautiful park with his eyes shut tight, there's no need to imagine trees, flowers, deer, birds, and sky; we merely need to open our eyes and realize what is already here, who we already are - as soon as we stop pretending we're small or unholy." — Bo Lozoff

89. "[Mindfulness] is not concerned with anything transcendent or divine. It serves as an antidote to theism, a cure for sentimental piety, a scalpel for excising the tumor of metaphysical belief." — Stephen Batchelor

90. "Let the breath lead the way." — Sharon Salzberg

91. "We too should make ourselves empty, that the great soul of the universe may fill us with its breath." — Laurence Binyon

92. "Stop, breathe, look around and embrace the miracle of each day, the miracle of life." — Jeffrey A. White

93. "What is it about our expectations, plans, or ideas that hold such sway over us? It is as if we've written a script for a play of our lives that runs about a month ahead of actual life; if reality varies from what we've created in our minds we disengage or pout." — Holly Sprink

94. "We may be living past and future lives at the same time we are living this one." — Doug Dillon

95. "Collaboration is the essence of life. The wind, bees and flowers work together, to spread the pollen. Mindfulness gives us the opportunity to work with the cosmic collaboration." — Amit Ray

96. "Concentration is like a leash for our mind, keeping it under control and obedient and not giving it too much room to move as it wishes." — Evan Sutter

97. "Live in the mysterious. Accepting and being fully at peace with not knowing what's going to happen in the future will allow us to be fully present and more peaceful in the present." — Matthew Donnelly

98. "Compassion is not complete if it does not include oneself." — Allan Lokos

99. "To reteach a thing its loveliness is the nature of metta. Through loving kindness, everyone & everything can flower again from within." — Sharon Salzberg

100. "An open beginner's mind is a powerful tool for developing patience." — Allan Lokos

101. "The mind is just like a muscle - the more you exercise it, the stronger it gets and the more it can expand." — Idowu Koyenikan

102. "Without the ability to be present we are missing much of what the adventure has to offer." — Allan Lokos

103. "Mind is like a net, drawn by the needles of past and future. Mindfulness is the way for not getting stuck into that net." — Amit Ray

104. "Mindfulness is not the path of chasing. It is the path of beautification. When flowers blossom, the fragrance spreads, and the bees come." — Amit Ray

105. "Whatever it is you want in this life, be it material things, a place you want to be, or an experience you want to have, you must first make it real in the realm of your consciousness." — Brandi L. Bates

106. "When you have any sort of intense emotional reaction, you have a choice: look for proof that you should feel it even deeper or look for the thought process that is triggering the emotion. One takes you on a downwards spiral, while the other upwards. One breeds toxic patterns, the other awareness. The choice is yours." — Vironika Tugaleva

107. "When you open your mind, you open new doors to new possibilities for yourself and new opportunities to help others." — Roy Bennett

108. When we allow the mind to shut down we let things be as they are." — Matthew Donnelly

109. "Meditation is the art of silencing the mind so that you may hear the inklings of the Soul." — Manprit Kaur

110. "We cannot force the development of mindfulness." — Allan Lokos

111. "The future is always beginning now." — Mark Strand

112. "Why do they not teach you that time is a finger snap and an eye blink, and that you should not allow a moment to pass you by without taking joyous, ecstatic note of it, not wasting a single moment of its swift, breakneck circuit?" — Pat Conroy

113. "If you surrender completely to the moments as they pass, you live more richly those moments." — Anne Morrow Lindbergh

114. "We spend precious hours fearing the inevitable. It would be wise to use that time adoring our families, cherishing our friends and living our lives." -— Maya Angelou

115. "Seeking is endless. It never comes to a state of rest; it never ceases." — Sharon Salzberg

116. "It's good to have an end in mind but in the end what counts is how you travel." — Orna Ross

117. "Be happy in the moment, that's enough. Each moment is all we need, not more." — Mother Teresa

118. "Look at everything as though you were seeing it either for the first or last time. Then your time on earth will be filled with glory." — Betty Smith

119. "Life is a preparation for the future; and the best preparation for the future is to live as if there were none." — Albert Einstein

120. "Begin at once to live, and count each separate day as a separate life." - Seneca

121. "Waste not fresh tears over old griefs." — Euripides

122. "One can make a day of any size, and regulate the rising and setting of his own sun and the brightness of its shining." - John Muir

123. "Renew thyself completely each day; do it again, and again, and forever again." Henry David Thoreau

124. "I wish that life should not be cheap, but sacred. I wish the days to be as centuries, loaded, fragrant." - Ralph Waldo Emerson

125. "Try dying every day to your old self.. So that you emerge renewed and young again as the tired mind sheds its load." - Kristin Zambucka

126. "There is no better means of attainment to the spiritual life. Than by continually beginning again." - Saint Francis de Sales

127. "Living the past is a dull and lonely business; looking back strains the neck muscles, causing you to bump into people not going your way." — Edna Ferber

128. "The passing moment is all that we can be sure of; it is only common sense to extract its utmost value from it." - W. Somerset Maugham

129. "Slow down and enjoy life. It's not only the scenery you miss by going too fast - you also miss the sense of where you are going and why." -Eddie Cantor

130. "Always hold fast to the present. Every situation, indeed every moment, is of infinite value, for it is the representative of a whole eternity." - Johann Wolfgang von Goethe

131. "As you walk and eat and travel, be where you are. Otherwise you will miss most of your life." - Buddha

132. "To see a world in a grain of sand and heaven in a wild flower, Hold infinity in the palm of your hand and eternity in an hour." -William Blake

133. "Wanting to reform the world without discovering one's true self is like trying to cover the world with leather to avoid the pain of walking on stones and thorns. It is much simpler to wear shoes." — Ramana Maharshi

134. "Do what you can, with what you have, where you are" — Theodore Roosevelt

135. "If you feel lost, disappointed, hesitant, or weak, return to yourself, to who you are, here and now and when you get there, you will discover yourself, like a lotus flower in full

bloom, even in a muddy pond, beautiful and strong."— Masaru Emoto, The Secret Life of Water

136. "Don't let yesterday use up too much of today."— Cherokee Indian Proverb

137. "I tell you the past is a bucket of ashes." — Carl Sandburg

138. "When one door closes another door opens; but we so often look so long and so regretfully upon the closed door, that we do not see the ones which open for us." — Alexander Graham Bell

139. "It's but little good you'll do a-watering the last year's crops." — Mary Anne Evans

140. "In the carriages of the past you can't go anywhere." — Maxim Gorky

141. "If you wait for tomorrow, tomorrow comes. If you don't wait for tomorrow, tomorrow comes." — Senegalese Proverb

142. "God made the world round so we would never be able to see too far down the road." — Karen Blixen

143. "Life is all memory, except for the one present moment that goes by you so quickly you hardly catch it going." — Tennessee Williams

144. "When we lack mindfulness, we are like someone who builds a house out of ignorance. . . . The wind comes and blows it away." - The Jesus Sutras

145. "It is only possible to live happily-ever-after on a day-to-day basis." - Margaret Wander Bonnano

146. "Slight not what's near through aiming at what's far." — Euripides

147. "It's surprising how much memory is built around things unnoticed at the time." - Barbara Kingsolver"

148. Rejoice in the things that are present; all else is beyond thee." — Michel de Montaigne

149. "I got the blues thinking of the future, so I left off and made some marmalade. It's amazing how it cheers one up to shred oranges and scrub the floor." - D.H. Lawrence

150. "Nothing ever gets anywhere. The earth keeps turning round and gets nowhere. The moment is the only thing that counts." — Jean Cocteau

151. "With the past, I have nothing to do; nor with the future. I live now." — Ralph Waldo Emerson

152. "Seize from every moment its unique novelty, and do not prepare your joys." — André Gide

153. "Let us not look back in anger, nor forward in fear, but around in awareness." — James Thurber

154. "Children have neither past nor future; they enjoy the present, which very few of us do." — Jean de la Bruyere

155. "Speech is the mirror of the soul; as a man speaks, so he is." - Publilius Syrus

156. "I think over again my small adventures, my fears, those small ones that seemed so big, all those vital things I had to get and to reach, and yet there is only one great thing: to live and see the great day that dawns, and the light that fills the world." - Inuit Saying

157. "When we understand how precious each moment is, we can treat each breath, each moment, as a newborn baby."- Michelle McDonald

158. "Do every act of your life as if it were the very last act of your life." — Marcus Aurelius

159. "Forever is composed of nows." — Emily Dickinson

160. "When the mind, one-pointed and fully focused, knows the supreme silence in the Heart, this is true learning." - Sri Ramana Maharshi

161. "Constantly observe and study the workings of the Ego. Understand it to control and use it. Failing which, the Ego takes over the control. We are turned into monkeys under the control of our masters, our egos." - Unknown

162. "Today stretches ahead of you waiting to be shaped. You are the sculptor who gets to do the shaping. What today will be like is up to you." - Steve Maraboli

163. "Love the moment, and the energy of that moment will spread beyond all boundaries." - Corita Kent

164. "How many times have you noticed that it's the little quiet moments in the midst of life that seem to give the rest extra-special meaning?" - Fred Rogers

165. "Self-awareness is an act of self-kindness." - Reuben Lowe

166. "Try pausing right before and right after undertaking a new action, even something simple like putting a key in a lock to open a door. Such pauses take a brief moment, yet they have the effect of decompressing time and centering you." - David Steindl-Rast

167. "Make your meditation a continuous state of mind. A great worship is going on all the time, so nothing should be neglected or excluded from your constant meditative awareness." - Sri Ramana Maharshi

168. Time is the coin of your life. It is the only coin you have, and only you can determine how it will be spent. Be careful lest you let other people spend it for you."- Carl Sandburg

169. "When you mind is made up, there's no point trying to change it, but YOU still have a choice." - Reuben Lowe

170. "Why is it that when we follow our hearts, we also end up being paralyzed by fear? Following the heart is the easy part,

while the way we handle our fears makes the difference between Kings and Paupers." - Unknown

171. "The key is to trust your heart to move where your unique talents can flourish. This old world will really spin when work becomes a joyous expression of the soul." - Al Sacharov

172. "It is true that we are called to create a better world. But we are first of all called to a more immediate and exalted task: that of creating our own lives." - Thomas Merton

173. "Fear is a dark cloudy mist of ignorance. And Knowledge is like the Sun, in whose presence the dark cloudy mist disappears instantaneously, resulting in clarity of thought and profound wisdom." - Unknown

174. "Study how water flows in a valley stream, smoothly and freely between the rocks. Also learn from holy books and from wise people. Everything- even mountains, rivers, plants and trees- should be your teacher." - Morehei Ueshiba

175. "Rest is not idleness, and to lie sometimes on the grass under the trees on a spring day, listening to the murmur of water, or watching the clouds float across the sky, is by no means a waste of time." - John Lubbock

176. "If I had my life to live over again, I would ask that not a thing be changed, but that my eyes be opened wider." - Jules Renard

177. "A person may rise to the highest degree of contemplation even when busily occupied." - St Mary Euphrasia Pelletier

178. "Life is a great and wondrous mystery, and the only thing we know that we have for sure is what is right here and right now. Don't miss it." - Leo Buscaglia

179. "Without mindful awareness, the shadows of your past may haunt your present." - Reuben Lowe

180. "The point of diving in a lake is not immediately to swim to the shore, but to be in the lake. To luxuriate in the sensation

of water. You do not work the lake out; it is an experience beyond thought. Poetry soothes and emboldens the soul to accept mystery." - John Keats

181. "Everything that slows us down and forces patience, everything that sets us back into the slow circles of nature, is a help. Gardening is an instrument of grace." - Mary Sarton

182. "One day I will find the right words, and they will be simple." - Jack Kerouac

183. "In the space between your thoughts there is your truth." - Reuben Lowe

184. "Look not mournfully into the past, it comes not back again. Wisely improve the present, it is thine. Go forth to meet the shadowy future without fear and with a manly heart." - Longfellow

185. "Earth and sky, woods and fields, lakes and rivers, the mountain and the sea, are excellent schoolmasters, and teach some of us more than we can never learn from books." - John Lubbock

186. "In still moments by the sea life seems large-drawn and simple. It is there we can see into ourselves." - Rolf Edberg

187. "Live your life each day as you would climb a mountain. An occasional glance towards the summit keeps the goal in mind, but many beautiful scenes are to be observed from each new vantage point." - Harold B. Melchart

188. "Perhaps then, some day far in the future, you will gradually, without even noticing it, live your way into the answer." - Rainer Maria Rilke

189. "Life exists only at this very moment, and in this moment it is infinite and eternal, for the present moment is infinitely small; before we can measure it, it has gone, and yet it exists forever." - Unknown

190. "Need to be smart by existing. Need to be wise by living." - Unknown

191. "Life is like a taste of honey, sour, bitter, spice, salty. Hope you will taste the honey one day.......SOON !" - Unknown

192. "Trees are sanctuaries. Whoever knows how to speak to them, whoever knows how to ...listen to them, can learn the truth. They do not preach learning and precepts, they preach undeterred by particulars, the ancient law of life." - Herman Hesse

193. "Expecting is the greatest impediment to living. In anticipation of tomorrow, it loses today." - Seneca

194. "It is a mistake to look too far ahead. Only one link in the chain of destiny can be handled at a time." - Winston Churchill

195. "I don't think we are here for anything. We're just products of evolution. You can say, "Gee, your life must be pretty bleak if you don't think there's a purpose." But I'm anticipating a good lunch." - James Watson

196. "The next message you need is always right where you are." - Ram Dass

197. "Something precious is lost if we rush headlong into the details of life without pausing for a moment to pay homage to the mystery of life and the gift of another day." - Kent Nerburn

198. "Knowledge is knowing that we cannot know." - Ralph Waldo Emerson

199. "When we are in the midst of chaos, let go of the need to control it. Be awash in it, experience it in that moment, try not to control the outcome but deal with the flow as it comes." - Leo Babauta

200. "Once you stop clinging and let things be, you'll be free, even of birth and death. You'll transform everything...And you'll be at peace wherever you are." - Bodhidharma

201. "Be a lamp unto yourselves! Work out your liberation with diligence! Fill your mind with compassion!" - Buddha

202. "We see things not as they are, but as we are." - H.M. Tomlinson

Conclusion

Thanks again for purchasing this book. Hopefully you've learned what it means to be mindful and how to go about incorporating the exercises and techniques shown in this book into your every day life.

I've found being more mindful of myself and the situations I'm in has dramatically improved my life for the better. It took me a little time to get started. Meditation and staying still felt very foreign to me at first. However, once I got the ball rolling, really embraced the ideals of mindfulness, everything began to fall into place. Areas of my life I once struggled with, like relationships, began to blossom and I was able to embrace new opportunities with open arms as they came to me.

I hope you find the same success after reading this book.

Good luck! I wish you nothing but the best!

Made in the USA
San Bernardino, CA
07 May 2018